1 The Beginning of the World

In the beginning, God made the heavens and the earth!
Use the color code to discover a scene from God's creation.

Coloring Code		
• yellow	••• blue	••••• brown
•• red	•••• green	

BIG Idea

God created the world because God loves us.

Bible Text Genesis 1:1-31, 2:1-3

Key Verse God saw everything that he had made, and indeed, it was very good. Genesis 1:31

Find Genesis 1 in your Bible. Genesis is the first book in the Bible. Use the Bible verses listed below each box to help you draw pictures that tell about God's creation of the world.

Genesis 1:1-5	Genesis 1:6-8	Genesis 1:9-13

AND GOD SAW THAT IT WAS GOOD

2 Living With God's Promise

T D I B G I R A F F E
N I E E N K A N T K V
A G B E U C E O A A O
H O E B R U B N M N D
P A C X A D S E R G O
E T I G E R O V O A D
L E M A C X W A W R T
E M U N O I L R I O X
G O R F L A M B W O C

Can You Find...? Try to find some of the animals Noah invited on the ark. Use the words in this box:

Deer	Giraffe	Fox
Bee	Camel	Duck
Elephant	Kangaroo	Lamb
Ox	Frog	Raven
Gnu	Bear	Worm
Ant	Emu	Tiger
Dove	Snake	Owl
Rabbit	Bird	Mice
Lion	Cow	Goat

Bible Text Genesis 6-9

Key Verse I have set my bow in the clouds, and it shall be a sign of the covenant between me and the earth. Genesis 9:13

A Rainbow Promise

Work together to fill in the blanks with words from today's story.

God was pleased with ______ because Noah was __________ with God. God wasn't happy with the people in the world who were disobeying God's plan. God told Noah to build an _____ . "I am going to bring a _______ to destroy the earth," God said. "But I will make a ___________, or promise, with you and your family. Bring ____ of every living creature with you. I will save them too." The rain poured from the sky. The flood continued for _______ days and _______ nights. But God remembered ______ and everyone on the ark. After the rain stopped, the _______ dried up from the _______. God told Noah to bring everyone out of the ark. Then Noah built an _______ to worship God. God was pleased and said, "I will never send a _______ to destroy the earth again." And God set a __________ in the sky as a sign to remind people of God's ___________ or __________.

3 Faithful People

What Is It? Today's Bible story is about two of God's faithful people, Abraham and Sarah. Although they thought they were too old to have children, God had other plans! There are many Christian symbols that are reminders of hope, such as a cross, ship, lamb, and stars. The symbol of a large star surrounded by smaller stars reminds us of Abraham and his descendants—the people who came after him, including you! Connect the dots to create a hopeful symbol.

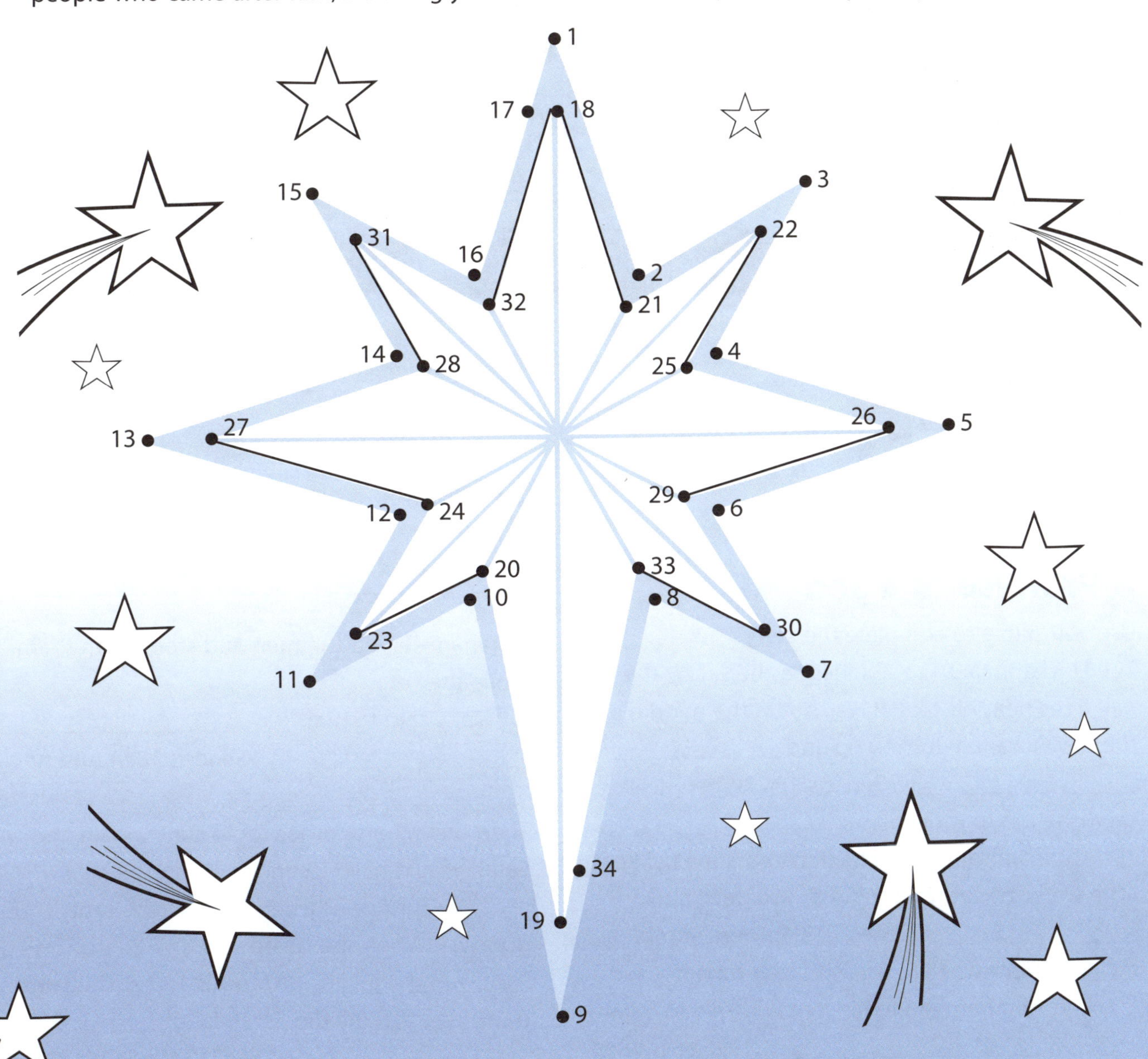

Big Idea

God's promises give us hope.

Bible Text Genesis 18:1-15, 21:1-7

Key Verse Is anything too wonderful for the Lord? Genesis 18:14

A Promise of a Son

Use your Bible to complete the story:

The Lord appeared to Abraham as he sat by the oak trees near his tent. It was hot in the middle of the day. Abraham looked up and ____________ __________________. (Genesis 18:2) When he saw them, he ran to meet them.

Abraham said, "My Lord, don't pass me by! Let a little water be brought to wash your feet, and ________________. (Genesis 18:4) Then let me _______(Genesis 18:5) that you may be refreshed."

And Abraham ran to his tent and said to Sarah, "_____________________________." (Genesis 18:6) Then Abraham had a servant prepare a calf, and Abraham served the men and stood with them while they ate.

They said to him, "________________________ __________________?" (Genesis 18:9) And he said, "____________________ _________." (Genesis 18:9) Then one man said he would come again and Sarah would have a son!

Now Sarah was listening from the tent doorway. When she heard this, ________________ __________________. (Genesis 18:12) The Lord said to Abraham, "Why did Sarah laugh? ______________ _________." (Genesis 18:14) When it is time, Sarah will have a son.

4 God Gives Us Courage

Hidden Picture Color the dotted spaces to see who is hiding in the reeds!

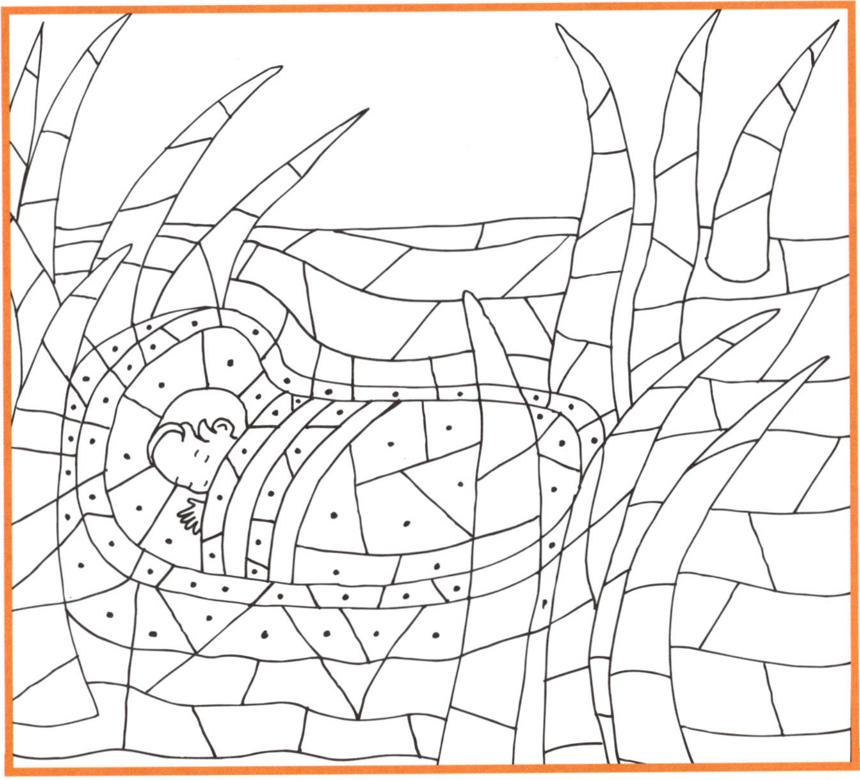

A Little History

Here's what happened before today's Bible story: Because of a famine, the Israelites moved to Egypt. Pharaoh, an Egyptian ruler, disliked the Israelites. Pharaoh decided they should be slaves. Then he decided all Israelite baby boys should be killed.

BIG Idea

God gives us courage to help others.

Words to Know

Papyrus – A tall plant that grows by the Nile River in Egypt.
Reeds – Tall grasses that grow in wet areas.
Pharaoh – A ruler of ancient Egypt.
Hebrews – Another name for the Israelite people.

Bible Text Exodus 2:1-10
Key Verse When the child grew up, she brought him to Pharaoh's daughter, and she took him as her son. She named him Moses, "because," she said, "I drew him out of the water." Exodus 2:10

Baby Moses is Rescued

Read today's Bible story from Exodus 2:1-10. Then answer these questions:

At first, what did the woman do with her baby boy?
(v. 2)____________________

What did she make the basket from?
(v. 3)______________________________

What did she do with the basket?
(v. 3)________________________________

What happened when Pharaoh's daughter went to the river?
(v. 5)________________

Who did she think the baby belonged to?
(v. 6) ____________________

How did the baby's sister help?
(vv. 7-8)________________________________

What did Pharaoh's daughter name the boy? Why?
(v. 10)______________________

THINK ABOUT IT

How would you have felt if you had been baby Moses' sister or brother?

5 Moses Trusts God

Finding the Way Help the Israelites find their way out of the wilderness!

Dear Diary,
Things are changing so fast! First Mother and Father hurried home. Moses, our leader, told us it was time to leave Egypt! So we packed our things and left. At first it was fun and exciting. But now people are grumbling. Are we lost? Even though God has led us with fire and a cloud, we don't know where we are! We are tired. And I am scared. Hannah

Israelite Press

Today's Weather:
Cloudy. Dark tonight, except for a pillar of fire.

If the Israelites had a newspaper account of their trip through the wilderness, it might have looked something like this:

Bible Text: Exodus 14:1-30

Key Verse: But Moses said to the people, "Do not be afraid, stand firm, and see the deliverance that the Lord will accomplish for you today." Exodus 14:13

READ ALL ABOUT IT!

Editorial

"Where are we going? Are we there yet?" These comments are heard throughout the crowd of weary Israelites as they follow Moses, a man God chose to lead them through the wilderness. With Pharaoh and his army in hot pursuit, the question this editor asks is, How long can this continue?

Israelite Update

Today, as the Israelites continue their journey through the wilderness, Pharaoh and his leaders wonder, "What have we done? Who will serve us now?" Acting quickly, Pharaoh's army mounted chariots (more than 600!) and began their pursuit of God's people. When the Israelites saw the army approaching, they cried out to God. But Moses spoke boldly, "Don't be afraid! Stand firm! See how God will protect you today!" Then God spoke to Moses: "Keep moving toward the sea. Lift your staff. The water will divide so my people can walk through."

Moses obeyed God and the people hurried safely through the sea. But when Pharaoh's army charged after them, their chariots stuck in the mud!

When God told Moses to stretch his hand over the water, it rushed back over the Egyptian army. But God's people were safe on the other side!

6 God Gives Us All We Need

Missing Foods Puzzle In Egypt, God's people had good food to eat. As they journeyed through the wilderness, they missed that good food. Find and circle the foods the Israelites missed eating while they were in the wilderness.

dates figs grapes	bread wine watercress	endive parsley cucumbers	lamb olives

k	l	o	n	p	z	w	a	f	g	x
m	c	d	f	o	a	m	b	m	r	s
b	e	t	o	l	a	m	b	u	a	t
a	n	m	i	i	d	c	w	a	p	x
f	i	g	s	v	b	u	u	p	e	y
a	w	a	t	e	r	c	r	e	s	s
d	a	t	e	s	e	u	n	n	o	t
x	o	c	q	l	a	m	t	d	u	n
b	c	g	f	h	d	b	k	i	f	w
m	p	a	r	s	l	e	y	v	x	t
a	h	c	a	g	h	r	b	e	i	h
k	d	j	s	l	m	s	y	l	e	a

Israelite Press

Today's Weather:
Continued cool and cloudy, with occasional bursts of light.

If the Israelites had a newspaper account of their trip through the wilderness, it might have looked something like this:

Bible Text: Exodus 16:1-18

Key Verse: So Moses and Aaron said to all the Israelites, "In the evening you shall know that it was the Lord who brought you out of the land of Egypt, and in the morning you shall see the glory of the Lord."
Exodus 16:6-7

READ ALL ABOUT IT!

Editorial

Amazing! God rescued the Israelites at the Red Sea, but still they continue to complain. This editor wonders: When will the Israelites truly put their trust in God?

Israelite Update

Today in the wilderness, the grumbling continues among the weary travelers. The biggest complaint? Most say it is the lack of good food. "We always had fresh vegetables and fruits in Egypt," several people remarked. "We were never hungry there!"

God heard the complaints and told Moses, "I will make it rain bread from heaven! Each morning the people will gather my special bread. But they must gather only enough for that day. Also, I will send quail to provide meat for the evening meal."

News spread of God's plan. The next morning the Israelites awoke to frosty dew covering the ground. Upon closer inspection, they discovered that the "dew" was the special bread or manna God had promised. The manna was plentiful, as were the quail that came in the evening. But some greedy people took more than they needed. The extra portions rotted and crawled with worms!

The question still remains: When will the Israelites learn to trust God?

7 God Is Always With Us

God's Promises For Us There are many places in the Bible where God promises to love and care for us. God makes other promises, too. Find these verses in your Bible and draw a line to match them to the promises listed here:

Psalm 37:5	The Lord watches over all.
1 Peter 5:7	God will pour down blessings.
Psalm 145:20	As God was with Moses, God will be with you.
Malachi 3:10	Trust God and God will act.
Joshua 1:5	God cares for you.

A City's Walls Today's Bible story is about the city of Jericho. It was common in Bible times to build large walls around a city to protect the citizens and animals that lived inside. Complete this drawing of a typical Bible times city.

Bible Text Joshua 6:1-20

Key Verse Be strong and courageous; do not be frightened or dismayed, for the Lord your God is with you wherever you go. Joshua 1:9

The Jericho Journal

Today the task the Lord gave me is complete!

After Moses died, the Lord promised me, "I will be with you." Then the Lord told me to march with all the people around the city wall of Jericho. We did—once a day for six days. Seven priests blowing trumpets led the way.

Today, the seventh day, I woke everyone at sunrise. We began the march, but before the trumpets blew I ordered everyone to shout! I said, "The Lord has given you this city! Everything in it must be destroyed as an offering to God. Only Rahab and her family, who hid our spies, will be saved. Beware—don't take anything from the city! Set aside all things made of precious metals as a gift for the Lord."

Then the trumpets blew, the people shouted, and the walls crumbled and fell! Everyone in the city perished, except for Rahab and her family. It was a long, difficult day, but God was surely with us.

Joshua

8 Called By God

Who Heard God's Call? Many people have been called by God. Sometimes they have heard God's voice or have had a dream in which God speaks to them. When God calls someone, his or her life changes. Find these Bible verses and read about some of the Bible people God called. Write the verses by the pictures they match.

Genesis 22: 1-14
Genesis 46:1-7
Exodus 3:1-8
1 Samuel 3: 1-10
Acts 9:10-16

Bible Text Judges 6:1-24

Key Verse The angel of the Lord appeared to him and said to him, "The Lord is with you."
Judges 6:12

BIG Idea

God wants us to worship and serve only God.

God Calls Gideon

Use your Bible to complete today's story from Judges 6:1-24:

The Israelites did what was ____________ in the sight of the Lord, and the ______________ gave them into the hand of Midian seven __________. The hand of Midian prevailed over ________; and because of Midian the Israelites ____________ for themselves hiding places in the mountains, ______________ and strongholds. (Judges 6:1-2)

When the Israelites cried to the Lord on account of the Midianites, the Lord sent a ______ __________ to the Israelites; and he said to them, "Thus says the __________, the God of Israel: I led you up from __________, and brought you out of the house of ____________; and I delivered you from the hand of the ______________, and from the hand of all who oppressed you, and drove them out before you, and gave you their ____________; and I said to you, 'I am the ___________ your God; you shall not pay ______________to the gods of the Amorites, in whose land you live.' But you have not given heed to my _________." (Judges 6:7-10)

The _________ of the ___________ appeared to (Gideon) and said to him, "The ____________ is with you, you ________ warrior." Gideon answered him, "But sir, if the Lord is __________ us, why then has all this happened to us?" (Judges 6:12-13)

Then the Lord turned to him and said, "_______ in this might of yours and ___________ Israel from the hand of Midian; I hereby commission you." (Judges 6:14)

9 Faithful Friends

Words to Live By The words hidden here remind us of what is important to a friend. Color the dotted spaces to see the words.

Friendly proverbs

Proverbs is a book filled with wise sayings that help us live in ways that please God and others. Find the following proverbs in your Bible. Then write a summary of each one.

Proverbs 17:9 ______________________________

Proverbs 18:24 ______________________________

Proverbs 19:4 ______________________________

BIG Idea

God teaches us to be faithful friends.

Bible Text Ruth 1:1-22

Key Verse "Where you go, I will go; Where you lodge, I will lodge; your people shall be my people, and your God my God." Ruth 1:16

Read the story of Ruth and Naomi from your Bible. Then, on a separate piece of paper, write what the characters might have said in the scenes pictured.

Ruth and Orpah are married to Naomi's sons. (Ruth 1:1-4)

Naomi's sons die. (Ruth 1: 5)

The women prepare to move to Naomi's hometown, Bethlehem.

Later, Naomi tells Orpah and Ruth to stay in Moab. Orpah agrees, but Ruth does not.

10 God Calls Samuel

Hearing God's Call Sometimes when God calls people, they pretend not to hear. You can read about one such person in the book of Jonah. Connect the dots to discover a famous symbol of Jonah's story.

BIG Idea

God calls us to be truthful.

Bible Text 1 Samuel 3: 1-18

Key Verse "Speak, Lord, for your servant is listening." 1 Samuel 3:9

Characters: Narrator, Samuel, Eli, Voice of God

Samuel Hears God's Call

Narrator: Hannah, Samuel's mother, promised God that her son would serve in the temple. Samuel loved God, and he helped Eli, a priest in the temple. One night Samuel heard someone call him.
God: Samuel!
Narrator: Samuel hurried to Eli's room.
Samuel: Here I am, for you called me!
Eli: Hrmph? What? I didn't call you. Go back to bed.
Narrator: Samuel went back to bed. Then he heard someone calling him again.
God: Samuel!
Samuel: This time it must be Eli.
Narrator: Samuel jumped out of bed and hurried to Eli's room.
Samuel: Here I am, for you called me!
Eli: What? I didn't call you. Now go back to bed!
Narrator: Samuel did as Eli said, but once again he heard someone calling. So he went back to Eli.
Samuel: Eli? It's me… Samuel! I know you called me this time!
Narrator: This time Eli wondered if God was calling Samuel's name.
Eli: Samuel, go back to bed. This time when someone calls you, say, "Speak, Lord, your servant is listening."
Narrator: So, Samuel went back to bed.
God: Samuel! Samuel!
Samuel: Speak, Lord, your servant is listening!
Narrator: God told Samuel about things that would happen to Eli's family. Samuel listened to God, and as he grew, people listened to him because he was one of God's prophets.

11 David and Goliath

A Different Way to Measure Not all countries use the same type of measurements. Some use inches and feet, while others use centimeters and meters. During Bible times, people measured things in another way. Use this chart and a ruler to help you determine how Bible measurements match up to measurements you use today.

Inches 1 2 3 4 5 6

Common Biblical Measurements Chart

A handbreadth = 4 fingers
A span = 3 handbreadths
A cubit = 2 spans (about 17 ¾ inches or 45 cm)

First, use a ruler to measure how wide 4 fingers of your hand are.
My handbreadth = ______________inches/cm
Now multiply your handbreadth by 3 to find a span.
My span = ___________________ inches/cm
Next, multiply your span by 2.
What did you get? _____________ inches/cm
This answer is your cubit measurement. How close are you to 17 ¾ inches (45 cm)?

Use Bible measurements to measure:
Your foot: ____________________
A doorway: ____________________
A friend's height: ___________

1cm 2 3 4 5 6 7 8 9 10 11 12 13 14 15 16 17 18

Bible Text 1 Samuel 17:4-11, 32-50

Key Verse David said, "The Lord, who saved me from the paw of the lion and from the paw of the bear, will save me from the hand of this Philistine." 1 Samuel 17:37

BIG Idea

God wants us to stand up for others.

Listen to the story of David and Goliath with your class, or read it in 1 Samuel 17:4-11, 32-50. Then number the following pictures in the order in which they happen in the story. Write a caption by each picture describing the scene. The first one has been done for you.

Goliath challenged the Israelites to fight him.

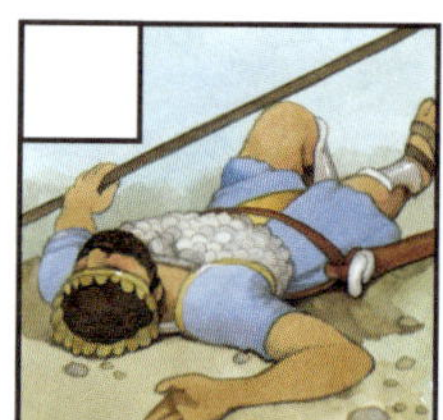

12 Daniel in the Lions' Den

Trusting God Daniel, one of God's faithful people, trusted God. He even trusted God to keep him safe in a den of lions! The people pictured here also trusted God, even when it was hard to do. Read about them in the Bible passages and then write their names in the space provided.

Genesis 6:11-17

Jonah 1:17

Acts 16:22-25

1 Samuel 17:4-11, 32-50

Genesis 37:23-28

Luke 1:26-38

Big Idea

God keeps us safe.

Bible Text Daniel 6:1-28

Key Verse I make a decree, that in all my royal dominion people should tremble and fear before the God of Daniel: For he is the living God, enduring forever. Daniel 6:26

A Man of Faith

Many years ago there lived a faithful man of God named Daniel. Daniel prayed three times each day, thanking God for watching over him.
Daniel had an important job. He was an advisor to the king. The king was pleased with Daniel's work. This made the other officials who worked for the king jealous. So they convinced the king to make a law that no one could pray to anyone but the king for 30 days. Anyone who broke the law would be thrown into a den of hungry lions!

Although Daniel wanted to obey the king, he did not stop praying to God.

When the king's officials saw Daniel praying to God, they hurried to tell the king. This news made the king very sad. He didn't want to throw Daniel to the lions.

As soldiers led Daniel away, the king said, "I hope your God saves you!" All that night, the king worried about Daniel. When the sun finally rose, the king hurried to the lions' den and called to Daniel. To his great surprise, Daniel answered!
Daniel said, "My God sent an angel and shut the lions' mouths so they would not hurt me."
The king was very happy that Daniel was alive. He said, "We will worship the God who saved Daniel!"

13 The Peaceful Kingdom

What the Bible Says About Peace

God wants everyone to live in peace. Read about God's peace from your Bible. Then summarize these verses:

proph et (prof' it)
tells about God's plan for the future
an inspired leader or teacher

Luke 2:14 ______________________

John 14:27 ______________________

Romans 5:1 ______________________

Galatians 5:22 ______________________

1 Peter 3:11 ______________________

Job 22:21 ______________________

What Is a Prophet?

Isaiah was a prophet from Old Testament times. The book of Isaiah tells about the coming of the Messiah and how one day the world will live in peace.

Big Idea

God promises us peace.

Bible Text Isaiah 11:1-9

Key Verse: They will not hurt or destroy on all my holy mountain; for the earth will be full of the knowledge of the Lord as the waters cover the sea. Isaiah 11:9

The Peaceful Kingdom

THE PEOPLE WHO WALKED IN DARKNESS HAVE SEEN A GREAT LIGHT. (ISAIAH 9:2)

THE SPIRIT OF THE LORD SHALL REST ON HIM. (ISAIAH 11:2)

THE WOLF SHALL LIVE WITH THE LAMB, THE LEOPARD SHALL LIE DOWN WITH THE KID, THE CALF AND THE LION AND THE FATLING TOGETHER, AND A LITTLE CHILD SHALL LEAD THEM. THE COW AND THE BEAR SHALL GRAZE... THE LION SHALL EAT STRAW LIKE THE OX. THE NURSING CHILD SHALL PLAY OVER THE HOLE OF THE ASP, AND THE WEANED CHILD SHALL PUT ITS HAND ON THE ADDER'S DEN. (ISAIAH 11:6-8)

FOR A CHILD HAS BEEN BORN... HE IS NAMED WONDERFUL COUNSELOR, MIGHTY GOD, EVERLASTING FATHER, PRINCE OF PEACE. (ISAIAH 9:6)

THEY WILL NOT HURT OR DESTROY ON ALL MY HOLY MOUNTAIN; FOR THE EARTH WILL BE FULL OF THE KNOWLEDGE OF THE LORD AS THE WATERS COVER THE SEA. (ISAIAH 11:9)

14 Mary, Faithful Woman of God

Life in Bible Times Mary was probably a young girl in today's Bible story. Learn what life may have been like for her. Add stickers to finish the pictures. Mary's home likely had two rooms and a courtyard. At night or during bad weather, animals stayed in the courtyard. Mary would have filled lamps with olive oil to keep them burning. Furniture was scarce. Families slept on bedrolls. Like other Bible times girls, Mary helped prepare meals, pounding grain for bread and drawing water from the town well.

Bible Text Luke 1:26-56

Key Verse For nothing will be impossible with God. Luke 1:37

A Messenger Comes to Mary

Use these words to complete the story:
Word Box: Gabriel, Nazareth, Joseph, angel, greeting, praised, afraid, baby, son, Son, Holy Spirit, holy, Galilee, nothing, Lord, with, baby, impossible, servant, cousin, Elizabeth, Blessed, love, care, Jesus, Son

The angel ______________ came to Mary in the town of ______________ in ______________. Mary was engaged to marry ______________.

"Greetings! The ________ is __________ you!" the ___________ said. But Mary was startled by this ______________. "Don't be _____________, Mary, for you have pleased God! You will have a _________, a ____________. And you will name him ____________. He will be great—the ______________ of God."

BIG Idea

God works in the lives of people who are faithful.

"How can this be?" Mary asked.

The angel told Mary that the _________ ________ would come to her. "Your son will be ____________," Gabriel said. "For __________ is __________ for God."

Then Mary said, "Here I am, the ____________ of the Lord." And the angel left.

Mary thought about all the angel had said, then she went to see her __________, _________. Elizabeth was going to have a _____________ too.

"______________ are you, Mary," Elizabeth said, "for you will have God's ______________."

Then Mary ______________ the Lord for his great __________ and ____________.

15 Jesus Is Born

Christmas Find One of the happiest days we celebrate is Christmas, the birth of Jesus! Look carefully at this picture. What things can you find from this list? What other things do you see that remind you of Christmas?

donkey • angel • shepherd • baby • lamb • camel • gift

BIG Idea

Jesus is for everyone.

Bible Text Luke 2:1-20

Key Verse And she gave birth to her firstborn son and wrapped him in bands of cloth, and laid him in a manger, because there was no place for them in the inn. Luke 2:7

Read the Bible verses that are next to each box. Then draw a picture that shows a scene from the story.

Luke 2:1-5	Luke 2:8	Luke 2: 9-14

Session 1
Generosity
Session 2
Obedience
Session 3
Patience
Session 4
Responsibility
Session 5
Boldness
Session 6
Thankfulness
Session 7
Perseverance
Session 8
Obedience
Session 9
Loyalty
Session 10
Honesty
Session 11
Responsibility
Session 12
Honesty
Session 13
Peace
Session 14
Patience
Session 15
Joy
Session 6
Session 14
Session 14

MOSES TRUSTS GOD

Session 5

GOD GIVES US ALL WE NEED

Session 6

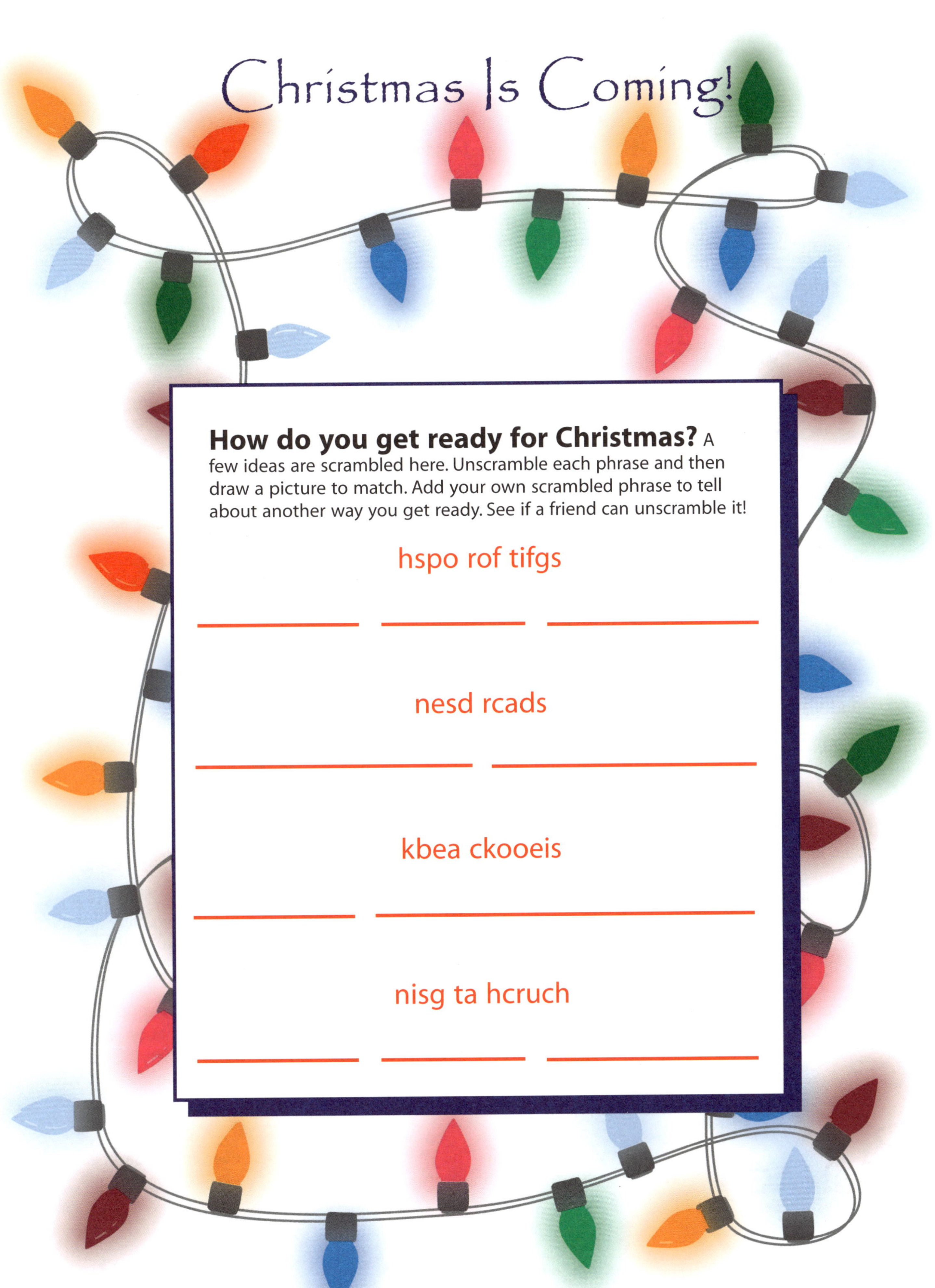

Christmas Is Coming!

How do you get ready for Christmas? A few ideas are scrambled here. Unscramble each phrase and then draw a picture to match. Add your own scrambled phrase to tell about another way you get ready. See if a friend can unscramble it!

hspo rof tifgs

__________ __________ __________

nesd rcads

__________ __________

kbea ckooeis

__________ __________

nisg ta hcruch

__________ __________ __________

Witness at Home!

Use these activities to nurture and celebrate faith at home.

KNOW

KNOW THE STORY

Ask your child to retell the story of Jesus' birth, then read it together from Luke 2:1-20. Talk about the night when Jesus was born. How would you have felt if you had been one of the shepherds who first heard the good news? How would you have felt after seeing Jesus in the manger?

GROW

GROW IN FAITH

There is something humbling about the fact that Jesus, God's Son, was born in a stable and laid in a manger filled with hay. Each year at Christmastime, we can regain some of the awe and wonder of the season, knowing that even in the most common circumstances, God is with us. Be watching for the ways that Jesus comes to you in the simple, daily parts of life.

emperor

decree

census

manger

Try This!

Make your own family Christmas cards! Have each family member draw or write about the most meaningful part of the season for him or her. Use a computer scanner or a photocopy machine to duplicate your work so you can send copies to extended family members and friends. What a great way to share the good news of the birth of the Christ child!

SHOW

SHOW SERVICE

"Project Angel Tree" provides gifts for children who have family members serving time in prison. Especially at this time of year, it can be very meaningful for families to participate in a project like this, providing a light in the darkest times of another family's life. For more information, visit www.angeltree.org. Or contact another charitable organization as a special way to serve Christ during this holiday season.

Thank you, dear Jesus, for this special time of the year. Even in the darkness of winter, your light still shines! **Amen**

Messengers

Locate the words in the word find puzzle.

```
O E A S T T A A P S N S O T L P B E S T B
E S T R O P K T R T I A N L B O V B T N T
L N A O N B S S T I N T E R N E T E N R S
P R O K S T K T S R H N S T B T N O I N B
R O S A R P T I K E A C B E B S B E E E S
O O B R O N N A O S O D A I E E O I T P O
D A V O T O C R O D D I I O T R N V E N A
R T T T S E S R B S A A B O S E P E T E E
I K N B A N I E R K S N A K S P I E S H P
I D T A P I I E I S O I R R O B T I E T S
O V P H O B H S N O E R P A R E N T S V A
N I S T H C I I E T I D K S D O B T D E N
I L R E A R B S P P S R E S S N T V D B S
H I E E T E C B B E O D E R T L R B E H E
S B T S N E L E N S E B I B L E V B H O K
R S V S R T H O B A P S A T T L A O T T P
```

Teachers
Radio
TV
Books
Internet
Parents
Pastors
Bible

Sharing the Good News Mary shared the good news of Jesus' birth with her cousin, Elizabeth. How do you share the good news of Jesus? Write or draw your ideas here.

Witness at Home!

Use these activities to nurture and celebrate faith at home.

KNOW

KNOW THE STORY

Read Luke 1:26-56 with your child from a Bible or use the version found on page 2 of this leaflet. Talk about the "Song of Mary," sometimes called "The Magnificat." How does Mary's song praise God?

patience

devotion

angel

GROW

GROW IN FAITH

Mary experienced an unexpected event in her life, yet she continued to trust and praise God. Have you ever had something unexpected happen to you? How did you react? What can you learn from Mary?

Try This!

In preparation for Christmas, and to honor the angel who gave Mary God's message, make a shell angel ornament to hang on your Christmas tree. Use a clean, white scallop shell for the base of the angel. Use craft glue or a hot glue gun to attach a bead to the smallest end of the shell for the angel's head, then glue on curled paper or ribbon for hair. Add a small wire halo and thread for hanging.

SHOW

SHOW SERVICE

When a family crisis happens, such as a serious illness or the loss of a caregiver's job, it can be difficult to face daily tasks, like preparing meals or doing laundry. Be aware of such times in the lives of your friends and neighbors, and find ways to help—perhaps by driving someone to a doctor appointment, inviting the children to play, or preparing an evening meal to share.

O God, you are so great! We can never understand all the plans you have for us. Help us look for your messages through your Word, in prayer, and from your faithful people. Thank you for sending your Son, Jesus, to teach us how to be faithful to you. **Amen**

Prophecy Puzzle

Review the Bible story from Isaiah as you complete this puzzle.

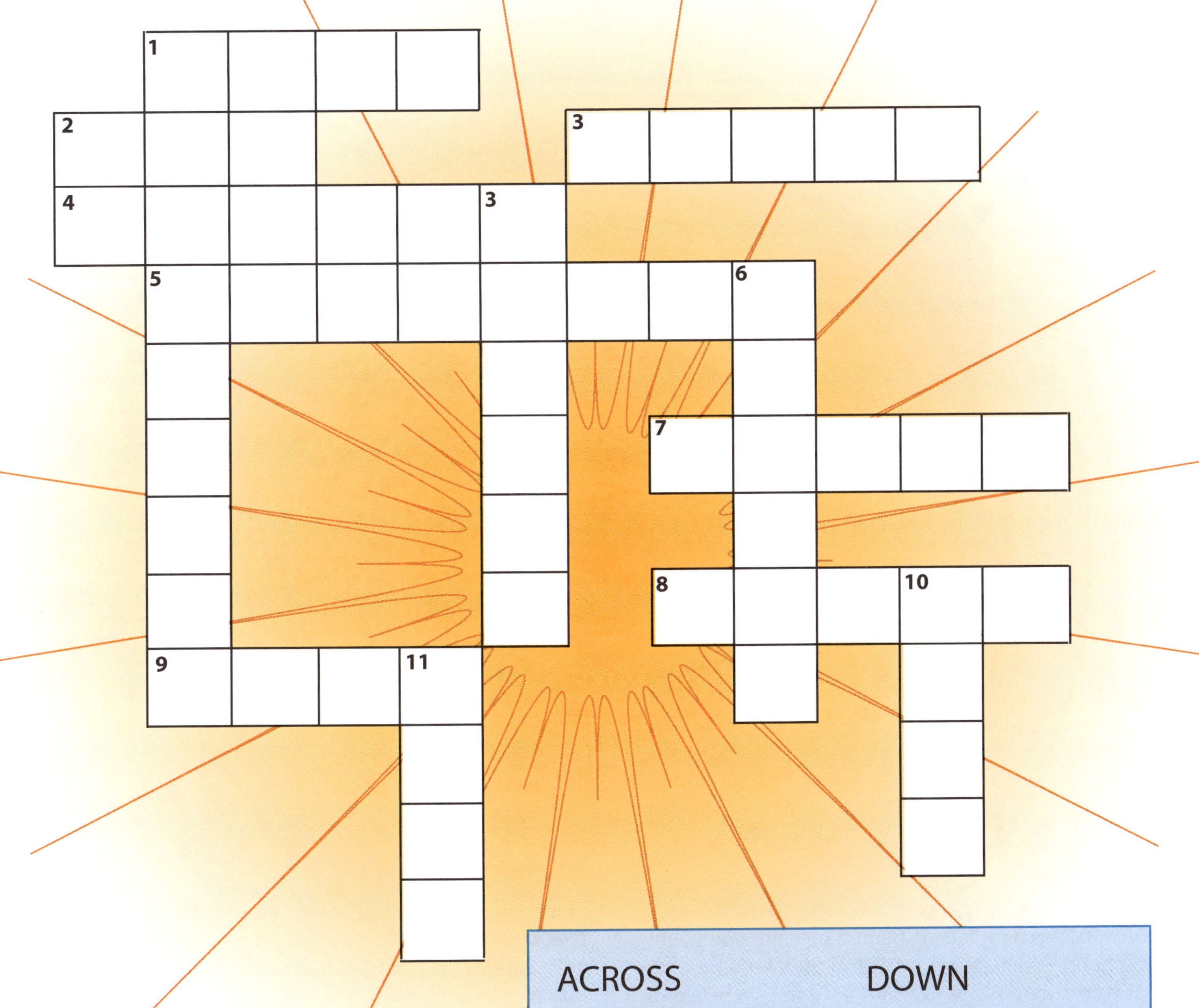

ACROSS

1. howls at the moon
2. another word for Lord
3. we live on this planet
4. reptiles that slither
5. not light, but ____
7. the opposite of dark
8. the opposite of war
9. a baby sheep

DOWN

1. _____counselor
3. the same as 4 across
6. "On them light has ____" (Isaiah 9:2).
10. a baby cow
11. I sleep in a cave

Witness at Home!

Use these activities to nurture and celebrate faith at home.

KNOW

KNOW THE STORY

Read Isaiah 9:1-7 and 11:1-9 with your child, or read through the verses printed on page 2 of this leaflet. Talk about places where peace is scarce today. Encourage your child to share his or her feelings about troubling situations at home, in your community, and in the world. Then share examples of peaceful situations and places. How does God give us peace, even in the midst of turmoil?

GROW

GROW IN FAITH

Peace often begins within. Find ways to allow peaceful moments to occur daily with your family, such as while driving in the car, sharing a meal, and preparing for bed. Peace in your family life may mean different things—quiet music, a flickering candle, or holding a pet. If you can help your child find peace in moments like these, peaceful moments can become a lifetime blessing.

prophet

justice

descendant

Try This!

Plan a family art night! Give everyone paper, markers, crayons, gel pens, paint, brushes, glitter glue, stamps, and any other art supplies you have on hand. Read Isaiah 11:1-9 and then let each person create his or her own version of a peaceful kingdom. Display the completed art in your home where it can remind everyone that peace begins with each of us.

Display a world map and identify countries or areas where there is war or unrest. Talk about the conflicts in these areas and include the people who live there in your daily prayers.

SHOW

SHOW SERVICE

There are many organizations around the world that promote peace. Your church may be affiliated with some of them. Find out which organizations you and your family could contribute to, either with volunteer time or with funds that will help others who are living in times of turmoil.

God of peace, show us how to make a difference in the world even when peace seems impossible. Thank you for loving and caring for us. **Amen**

How Do You Pray?

God wants people to pray at all times. There are many different types of prayers and many different ways to pray. Some people close their eyes, bow their heads, and fold their hands in prayer. Some people kneel quietly. Other people dance and sing their prayers. Read through the types of prayers listed here. When might you pray each type of prayer? Write your ideas in the spaces provided. Then write your own prayer to God!

Thanksgiving

A prayer of giving thanks to God.

Adoration

A prayer that worships and honors God.

Praise

A prayer to glorify God.

Petition

A prayer asking God for something.

Intercession

A prayer on behalf of, or for, others.

My Prayer

Write your own prayer here:

Witness at Home!

Use these activities to nurture and celebrate faith at home.

KNOW

KNOW THE STORY

Ask your child to tell you the story of Daniel in the den of lions. Why were the other officials jealous of Daniel? How did Daniel honor God each day? If you had been Daniel, would it have been hard to trust God? Share a time when it was especially hard for you to trust God.

GROW

GROW IN FAITH

Daniel prayed three times a day. How often do you pray? One way to grow in faith is with a daily prayer routine. Consider praying when you awake, at the evening meal, and again at bedtime. As your child sees you model daily prayer, he or she will be encouraged to make prayer a part of his or her daily life.

Witness WORDS

honesty

witness

Try This!

Does your family have a place for posting messages? For some families, it is the computer calendar. For others, it is a bulletin board or the refrigerator door. Consider adding a prayer list to your central spot. Head the prayer list with a weekly Bible verse to learn by heart. Leave space for everyone in the family to write or draw something to pray about. Provide stickers to add to those prayers that are answered. Refer to the list during your family prayer time.

SHOW

SHOW SERVICE

"Prayers of the church" are often included during a worship service. Such prayers may address the special needs of congregational members, extended families, friends, church leaders, and national or world leaders. Consider including these people in your family prayers as an act of loving service. Encourage each member of your family to choose one such person and offer prayers on his or her behalf during your family devotional time.

Jesus, we can only begin to know and understand our Creator through you. When we are afraid, help us feel safe in your presence. When we are tired, give us strength. When we are happy, share in our joy! **Amen**

People of God

This year your class has been learning about Bible people who were faithful to God. Unscramble their names below. Then think of people you know today who are faithful to God. Scramble the letters of their names and write them in the spaces provided.

Witness at Home!

Use these activities to nurture and celebrate faith at home.

KNOW

KNOW THE STORY

Review the story of David and Goliath with your child, using the text from 1 Samuel 17:4-11, 32-50 and the story boxes on page 2 of this leaflet. Talk about how God calls all people to stand up for others, regardless of their size or experience.

GROW

GROW IN FAITH

Do you ever feel inadequate in your faith? If David had stopped to think about his size and experience compared to Goliath's, he might have changed his mind about facing him in battle. But David trusted that God would be with him, just as God had been with him in other situations. Take time now to ask God to be with you as you face new challenges each day.

Witness WORDS

anointed

cubit

span

Try This!

Spending time together as a family can be a rare commodity in today's busy world. Find a favorite family game or two and have a "family game night" at least once a week. It doesn't matter what game you play, or who wins or loses—the important thing is spending time together!

SHOW

SHOW SERVICE

Responsibility is an important part of any family. How can your family take responsibility for the everyday things that need to happen in your home? Make a list of family chores. Perhaps place stars by your least favorite ones! Then talk about ways for everyone to pitch in and help with the chores. Consider switching chores for a week, or choose one day on which everyone works together to get most of them done.

Family Prayer

Dear Lord, thank you for stories about courage and responsibility, like David and Goliath. They remind us that you are with us in all situations, and that regardless of our skill or experience or size, you will help us accomplish great things through you! **Amen**

Picture Puzzle

Use the numbered letters in the word pictures to decode the sentence below.
What message do you discover?

1•12•7•12 13 2•11, 10•9•7 5•9•6 8•2•4•4•12•3 11•12.

" ____ "

Serving God

Samuel served God in the temple, a place of worship. Where and how do you serve God?

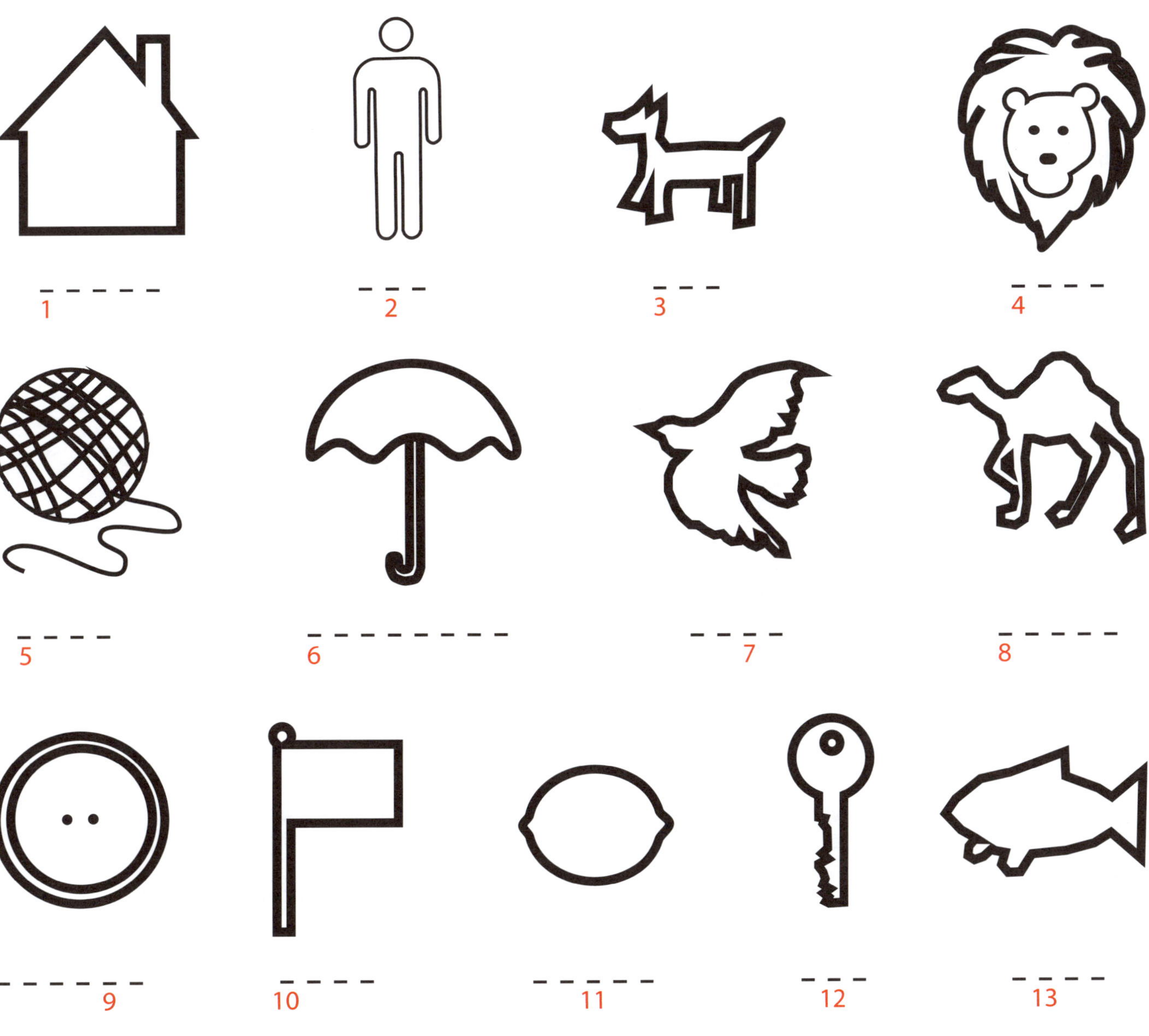

Witness at Home!

Use these activities to nurture and celebrate faith at home.

KNOW

KNOW THE STORY

Read 1 Samuel 3:1-18 with your child. Or read through the script on page 2 of this leaflet with your child and other family members. Talk about how Samuel learned from and worked with Eli, and how God called Samuel. Do you think Samuel was surprised when God called him? How would you have felt if you had been Samuel?

GROW

GROW IN FAITH

What has God called you to do? Although we may not feel we are called to do great things—things that will make the news or that everyone will know about—it is important to remember that God calls us in the little things we do each day. We need to remember that washing the dishes can be a calling that is just as important as preaching a great sermon.

respond

loyalty

Try This!

Make a family worship candle! Find a smooth glass jar or candle holder. Cut or tear colored tissue paper into small pieces. Spread clear-drying glue on the glass. Press and smooth tissue paper on it, overlapping some pieces for an interesting effect. Then coat the completed jar with more glue. Let dry. Place a small candle inside and light it during family devotions or prayer.

SHOW

SHOW SERVICE

The church is God's people working and worshiping together. Are there things you take for granted when you attend a worship service, such as worship folders to read, sharpened pencils to write with, refreshments to enjoy, and clean restrooms to use? Find out ways your family could help with tasks, such as folding bulletins, cleaning up after a worship service, or providing beverages and cookies for fellowship. Your help will be appreciated!

Thank you, Lord, for calling us to be in your family! Remind us to listen for your voice in all that we do and say. Help us share your message of peace and love with all of the people we meet. **Amen**

What Would You Do?

It isn't always easy to live in friendly ways. Read these stories, then write what you would do.

No one wants to sit with Selma on the school bus. "She dresses weird," the kids whisper as they pass her by. "And her hair looks terrible!" Now you are almost to Selma's row. There is an empty seat next to her.

You ____

____.

Tad is excited! His new friend, Brian, gets to spend the night! "By the way, Tad," Mom says. "Tell Brian we can take him home after church tomorrow." Uh-oh. Tad knows that Brian and his family don't go to church. If you were Tad, what would you do?

____

____.

Bridget works at a fast food restaurant. She works hard, but the line of customers moves slowly. As you wait in line, some boys make unfriendly comments about Bridget. And the woman she is serving yells at her. It's your turn to order next.

You ____

____.

Witness at Home!

Use these activities to nurture and celebrate faith at home.

KNOW

KNOW THE STORY

Read Ruth 1:1-22 with your child. Talk about the friendship that Ruth and Naomi shared. Does your family share that kind of friendship? Is it hard or easy to be friends with the people in your family? If not, how can God help?

GROW

GROW IN FAITH

The Witness Words for this session are *faithfulness* and *friendship*. What are the characteristics of a faithful friend? When are you a faithful friend to others? How is God a faithful friend in your life?

faithfulness

friendship

Try This!

Make friendship bracelets as a reminder of God's love for your family! Let everyone choose his or her favorite colors of embroidery floss or yarn. You will need three different colors for each bracelet. Tie the strands together at one end, then braid them. Tie a knot at the other end when the braid is long enough to tie around your wrist. Help your child find Ecclesiastes 4:9-12 in a Bible. Read what this passage has to say about friendship.

SHOW

SHOW SERVICE

There are many retirement centers and assisted living homes where some of the residents never have visitors. It can be pretty lonely. If there is a center like this in your community, why not "adopt" a resident? You and your family could send cards, stop by for a visit, or share special days and holidays with someone who otherwise might be alone.

Thank you, Jesus, for the friends in our lives—those we know today and those you will bring into our lives in the future. Like Ruth, help us learn to live as faithful friends every day, especially with the members of our family. **Amen**

They Answered God's Call

God calls people to do special things. Sometimes God calls us through the Bible. Sometimes God calls us through dreams. Sometimes God calls us through other people, such as parents, pastors, or teachers. Read the following riddles. Place the sticker that pictures each person next to his or her story:

I lived in Calcutta, India. God called me and other nuns to help people who were sick and dying. Who am I?

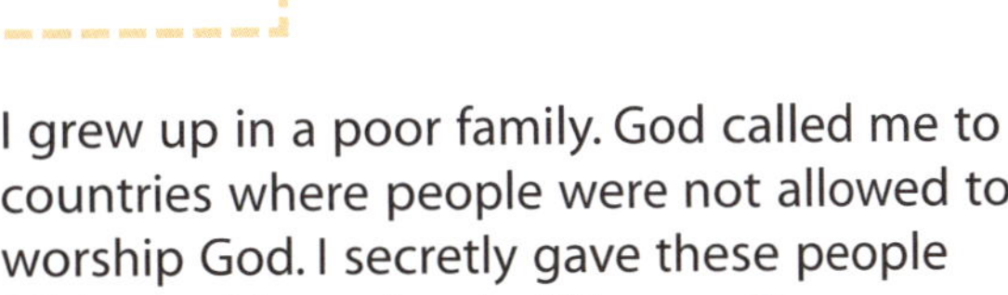

I grew up in a poor family. God called me to countries where people were not allowed to worship God. I secretly gave these people Bibles and hymnbooks. Who am I?

I lived in Holland during World War II. God called my family to help Jewish people hide from Nazi soldiers. Because of this, we were arrested and sent to a prison camp. After the war, I shared God's love with everyone I met. Who am I?

God called me to share the good news in large stadiums around the world. Through these "crusades" many people have learned about God. Who am I?

Bible Verse Scramble

heT leang fo eht odrL pepaarde ot mih dan isad ot mhi, "eTh rdoL si tiwh oyu." Judges 6:12

Unscramble this Bible verse and write it correctly here:

Witness at Home!

Use these activities to nurture and celebrate faith at home.

KNOW

KNOW THE STORY

Ask your child to tell the story of Gideon's call in his or her own words. Then look at the story as it appears on page 2 of this leaflet. How did God call Gideon? How does God call us today?

GROW

GROW IN FAITH

As we go about our daily lives, there may be times when we feel that we haven't heard from God for a long time. There is a saying that reads, "If there is a space between you and God, guess who moved?" Part of hearing God's call is taking time to slow down and listen. Remember to allow time for those quiet spaces in your day.

Witness WORDS

proclaim

worship

Try This!

Sometimes we forget that we have been called as children of God. Find or purchase a mirror in a plain frame. As a family, decorate the frame using paints, glue, sequins and beads, or natural objects such as pinecones or seashells. Write "I am a child of God!" somewhere on the frame. Display the mirror where everyone in your family can look into it and remember to serve and worship God!

SHOW

SHOW SERVICE

All around the world there are people who, for one reason or another, can't live in their homes. Homeless people exist in every society, and are often cold, tired, and hungry. Contact an agency or organization in your community that helps homeless people. Perhaps you can initiate or participate in a food, blanket, or clothing drive. Many times, a life of service begins at home.

Faithful God, thank you for calling us as your children! Help us to remember and honor all of the people you have called throughout history. Help us remember that you promise to always be with us, just as you promised Gideon to always be with him. **Amen**

You Are The Reporter!

Pretend you are a news reporter. Write the answers to the questions printed here. Use your Bible to help you. Draw a picture to show your version of the events in the story.

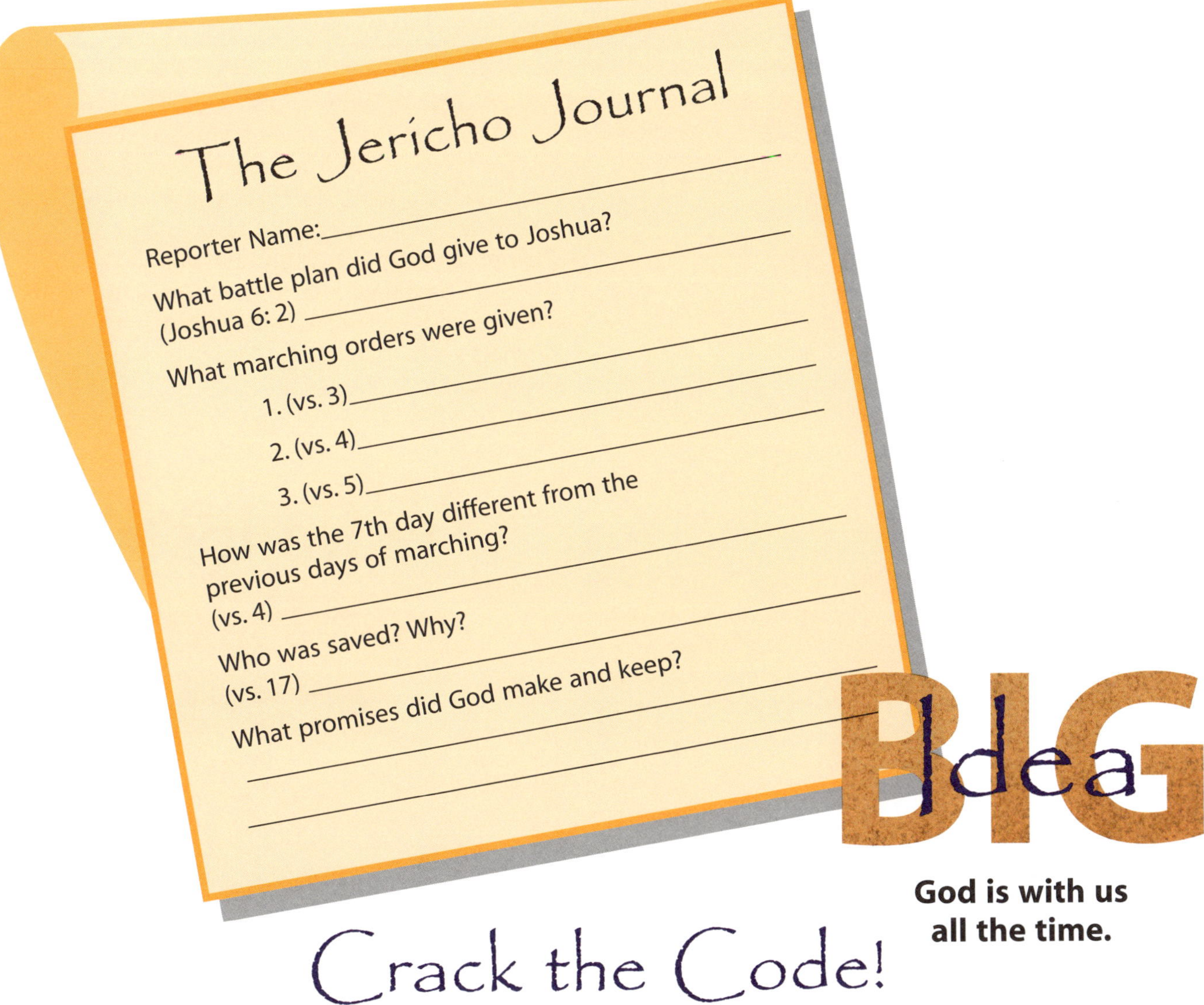

The Jericho Journal

Reporter Name: ____________

What battle plan did God give to Joshua? (Joshua 6: 2) ____________

What marching orders were given?

1. (vs. 3) ____________
2. (vs. 4) ____________
3. (vs. 5) ____________

How was the 7th day different from the previous days of marching? (vs. 4) ____________

Who was saved? Why? (vs. 17) ____________

What promises did God make and keep?

____

____

God is with us all the time.

Crack the Code!

Decode this Bible verse by numbering the letters of the alphabet 1-26 (A = 1). Then write a letter above each number.

2•5 • 19•20•18•15•14•7 • 1•14•4 • 3•15•21•18•1•7•5•15•21•19 ;

4•15 • 14•15•20 • 2•5 • 6•18•9•7•8•20•5•14•5•4 • 15•18 • 4•9•19•13•1•25•5•4,

6•15•18 • 20•8•5 • 12•15•18•4 • 25•15•21•18 • 7•15•4

9•19 • 23•9•20•8 • 25•15•21 • 23•8•5•18•5•22•5•18 • 25•15•21 • 7•15.

Joshua 1:9

Witness at Home!

Use these activities to nurture and celebrate faith at home.

KNOW

KNOW THE STORY

Look through today's leaflet with your child, reviewing the Bible story about Joshua and Jericho. How might Joshua have felt when he first heard God's plan for taking Jericho? How might the people have felt when Joshua told them about the plan? Joshua chose to trust God and persevere, even when faced with a plan that may have seemed likely to fail. Does God ever ask us to follow a plan that will fail?

GROW

GROW IN FAITH

God promises to be with us all the time. To know God's promises is to know God's peace. Think about a time when your family experienced a crisis or knew someone else who was experiencing a crisis. How were the promises of God a comfort during that time? How did your faith grow as a result?

perseverance

courage

Try This!

Build a city! Use a Bible dictionary, concordance, and other reference materials to help you plan, draw, and construct a model of a Bible time city. Gather necessary materials from around the house or at a craft store. This could be an ongoing project of great interest to your child and will utilize creative problem solving, math, and organizational skills.

SHOW

SHOW SERVICE

People who serve others in active ways, such as those who participate in a mission trip or those who volunteer with an organization such as Habitat for Humanity, often remark that they feel blessed by those whom they serve. If there is a local chapter of Habitat for Humanity in your community, find out how your family might participate in a future building project.

O Lord! We don't always understand the plans you have for us, but your promise to be with us at all times is clear. Help us keep your promises in mind as we go through our busy days and weeks. **Amen**

Psalm of Thanksgiving

The Book of Psalms can be found in the middle of the Bible. The Psalms include many prayers of thanksgiving. Find Psalm 138:1-3 in your Bible. Fill in the missing words below. Then use this psalm as a prayer today!

I give you ________, O Lord, with my whole ________;
I bow down toward your ________ temple and give ________ to
your name for your ________ ________ and your ____________;
for you have exalted your ________ and your word above
____________. On the day I ________, you ____________ me,
you increased my strength of soul.

What Are You Thankful For?

Draw or write about the things you are thankful for.
Remember to name these things when you pray!

God gives us what we need.

Witness at Home!

Use these activities to nurture and celebrate faith at home.

KNOW

KNOW THE STORY

Read through today's Bible story with your child from Exodus 16:1-18. Then read the newspaper account found on page 2 of this leaflet. Why were the people complaining in today's story? Do you think most people are ever satisfied with what they have, or are they always wanting more? What is the difference between "wants" and "needs"? What "needs" does God provide in your life?

GROW

GROW IN FAITH

What does it mean to be thankful? Thankfulness is something we often think about during the Thanksgiving holidays, but not as often during our daily lives. Do you offer thanks to God in your daily prayers, or do you usually ask God for something instead? How can we remember to thank God for providing all we need?

Witness WORDS

survive

thankfulness

manna

Try This!

Bake bread! Does your family have a favorite bread recipe? Prepare a special meal together that includes your favorite bread and perhaps a simple soup. Or purchase frozen bread dough from a grocery store. Thaw the dough according to package directions and then divide it into pieces for each family member. Have each person form the dough into the first initial of his or her name. Follow package directions for baking the bread. Enjoy!

SHOW

SHOW SERVICE

Sharing a meal is sometimes referred to as "breaking bread together." This phrase can also remind us of when we "break bread" with other Christians during the sacrament of Holy Communion. Many social events today, as in Bible times, are centered on the sharing of food. Is there a community supper or homeless shelter where your family could volunteer to prepare and serve a meal? Check with church leaders to see what opportunities are available.

Thank you, God, for daily bread,
And for the roof above my head.
Keep us safe and dry and warm,
Protect us all from every harm. **Amen**

You Were There!

It was an exciting time for the Israelites. But it was a scary time, too. Write about today's Bible story as if you were there. Circle the person listed here who you will pretend to be as you write, or add someone new to the list. Draw a "photograph" in the box that shows you in the story.

- **mother**
- **grandfather**
- **16-year-old girl**
- **10-year-old boy**
- **other** ____________

Witness at Home!

Use these activities to nurture and celebrate faith at home.

KNOW

KNOW THE STORY

Read through today's Bible story with your child from Exodus 14:1-30. Then read the "Israelite Press" found on page 2 of this leaflet. Why did the people begin to lose their trust in God? Have you ever lost your trust in God? What happened? How did you begin to trust God again?

GROW

GROW IN FAITH

Sometimes we can be so impatient! It is often hard for both children and adults to wait. We want God to give us answers and act on our prayers right now! It is important to help children know that our timing can be different than God's timing. Even though it may feel like God is answering a prayer request with "No," the answer may really be "Wait."

Witness WORDS

plague

slavery

trust

Try This!

Make an ocean! Ocean waves are a powerful force that many people experience with awe. Work together to demonstrate the power and beauty of ocean waves. Choose a clear plastic beverage bottle and fill it halfway with water. Then fill it nearly to the top with vegetable oil and a few drops of blue food coloring. Place a small toy boat inside. Secure the lid. Tilt the bottle sideways, rocking it back and forth. Observe how the boat it tossed back and forth.

SHOW

SHOW SERVICE

Do you ever take your family for granted? Sometimes we are kindest to the people who don't live with us. And even though we may not be unkind to our family, we may not be as thoughtful as we could be. Talk about this with your family and then try a "kindness experiment." See how it feels to treat everyone in your family as you treat friends, neighbors, teachers, and coworkers.

Family Prayer

Thank you, God, for guiding us through difficult times in our lives. When we encounter moments that seem too difficult to face, remind us of the Israelites in the wilderness. Help us trust in your strength when our faith seems weak.
Amen

Thinking About Courage

Who showed courage in today's Bible story?

Moses' mother showed courage by disobeying a bad law and saving her baby.

Pharaoh's daughter showed courage by rescuing a Hebrew baby.

Moses' sister showed courage by watching over her brother and offering to find someone to care for him.

The Bible has many stories about courageous people. But there are people today who show courage too:

- People with serious illnesses show courage when they endure treatments and surgeries.
- People who train to climb mountains or soar into outer space show courage.
- People who stand up for what they believe in show courage.

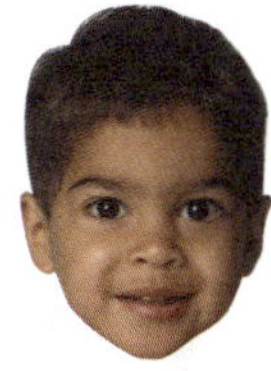

Who do you know who shows courage?________________________

Why do you think he or she is courageous? ________________________

When have you shown courage? ________________________

How does God help you be courageous? ________________________

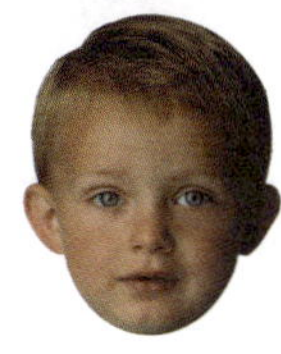

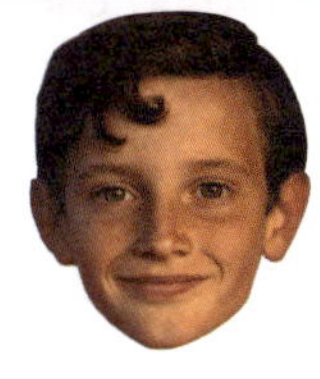

Witness at Home!

Use these activities to nurture and celebrate faith at home.

KNOW

KNOW THE STORY

Ask your child to retell the story of baby Moses to you. Talk about how difficult it must have been for the Hebrew parents who worried about their children. Look at photographs or keepsakes from your child's early years. Tell him or her stories about your family at that time.

Witness WORDS

reeds

famine

hospitality

prosper

GROW

GROW IN FAITH

Faith isn't something we can measure with a ruler or scale. But sometimes we sense our faith has grown when we worry less about something we used to worry about a lot. Or when we feel confident in a situation that once made us feel uncomfortable. Encourage your child to tell about times when his or her faith has felt weak and when it has grown stronger. Share your own faith stories as well.

Try This!

Weave a basket! Examine several baskets you have at home or visit a craft store with your child. What materials are the baskets made from? How do the weaving patterns differ? What is each basket's intended use? Experiment with basket designs by weaving thin strips of paper or ribbon into a mesh berry or produce basket. Fill the basket with wrapped cookies or other treats and offer it with hospitality to a neighbor or friend!

SHOW

SHOW SERVICE

When the Israelites began living in Egypt, they were shown hospitality. Hospitality is offering kindness and care to others. Make plans to offer hospitality to people in your community who show courage every day, such as firefighters and police officers. Consider bringing cookies or pizza to a local fire or police station as a gesture of thanks for all that these courageous people do in your community.

God, as we think about the story of baby Moses, help us remember courageous people in our lives today, especially *(name family members or friends)*. Thank you for blessing our lives with people who live in ways that reflect your care and concern. **Amen**

The Promises of God

The Bible includes many promises of God. One of God's promises is to hear all our prayers. Use your Bible to find and complete the verses listed here. Then read the circled letters. What does this promise say?__________ __________ __________

Ask me for _ _ _ _ _ _ _ _ ◯ in my name. (John 14:14)
Pray for _ _ _ _ _ ◯ _ _ _ _ _. (James 5:16)
Your Father will _ _ _ _ _ ◯ _ _ _ _. (Matthew 6:6)
Whenever we _ ◯ _ _ to God. (Deuteronomy 4:7)
Call to me, and I will _ ◯ _ _ _ _ you. (Jeremiah 33:3)
Ask for whatever you _ _ ◯ _. (John 15:7)
Before they call, I will _ _ _ ◯ _ _ _. (Isaiah 65:24)
We will _ _ _ _ _ _ _ ◯ mercy. (Hebrews 4:16)
I will _ _ _ _ _ ◯ them. (Psalm 91:15)
I will forgive their ◯ _ _ _. (2 Chronicles 7:14)
The _ ◯ _ _ _ _ comes to help us. (Romans 8:26)
The Lord is _ _ _ ◯ to all who call. (Psalm 145:18)
◯ _ _, and you will receive. (Matthew 7:7)
Those who lift up their hands in _ _ _ ◯ _ _ _. (1 Timothy 2:8)
Whatever you ask for in prayer, you will _ ◯ _ _ _ _ _ _ _. (Matthew 21:22)
The Lord ◯ _ _ _ _ _ _ _ them from all their troubles. (Psalm 34:17)

My Promises to God

What promises can you make to God? Write your ideas here:

Witness at Home!

Use these activities to nurture and celebrate faith at home.

KNOW

KNOW THE STORY

Look over the Bible story of Abraham and Sarah that your child read today. Talk about what it means to be "faithful people." How were Abraham and Sarah faithful? Share a time when you have been faithful, particularly when it seemed difficult to do. Talk about the ways God blesses us when we remain faithful to God's Word.

GROW

GROW IN FAITH

One way we grow in faith is by learning what God has to say in the Bible. Do you and your family have a regular time of Bible study? Do you memorize special Bible verses? Try memorizing one of these promises from God with your family this week: Matthew 11:28, Hebrews 13:5-6, 1 Peter 5:7, 1 John 1:9

Witness WORDS

promise

faithful

descendants

Try This!

Go stargazing! Check at a library for a book that tells about some of the basic constellations, such as the Big Dipper. Choose a clear night when the stars are shining brightly. Take along blankets, a thermos of a favorite warm drink, and snacks. Lie together on the blankets and try to identify all the stars you can. Choose an especially bright star and name it for your family.

SHOW

SHOW SERVICE

Are you aware of someone in your congregation or community who is expecting or adopting a child? Plan ways for your family to offer care during this time of transition by providing child care, home-cooked meals, or clothing and other needed items.

Family Prayer

Heavenly Father, we thank you for our family and for all families. Like Abraham and Sarah, help us be good and faithful people, sharing the stories of your love and promises with all of the people in our lives. **Amen**

Follow the Rules

It isn't always easy to follow the rules. In fact, sometimes it isn't even fun! Read the following stories and help Miguel, Verlecia, and Hailey decide what they should do.

Miguel is at a friend's house. The friend has a new video game, but it is one that Miguel's parents do not want him to play because it contains violence. What should Miguel do?

Verlecia did not finish her homework as she promised, so her parents told her she could not use the phone to call her friends. But she just has to tell her best friend, Amy, about her party next weekend! What should she do?

Hailey loves her new CD! But Mom told her she needs to clean her room or else! Maybe she can clean her room later, before Mom comes upstairs. What should she do?

Rainbow Prayer

Rainbows always have colors in exactly the same order—red, orange, yellow, green, blue, indigo, and violet. Sometimes people remember the color order like a person's name: ROY G. BIV. Add rainbow-colored stickers to this page, helping you write a prayer for each day of the week.

Sunday Thank you, God, for all ________________ that are red!

Monday God, I thank you today for yummy orange things that I love to eat, including ______________________.

Tuesday Thank you, Lord, for the bright yellow _______ and _______ that cheer me up.

Wednesday Creator, thank you for the green ______________ that color my world.

Thursday God, thank you for the blue ________ and the blue ________.

Friday Thank you, Jesus, for ______________________.

Saturday Thank you, Spirit, for violet ________________. Amen

Witness at Home!

Use these activities to nurture and celebrate faith at home.

KNOW

KNOW THE STORY

Read and review the story of Noah on page 2 with your child. What does the word covenant mean? *(Promise.)* Talk with your child about the importance of keeping promises. Share a time when you have experienced God's promises in your life.

GROW

GROW IN FAITH

This Bible story shows us someone who obeyed and trusted God. Obedience is an important faith trait to learn. What are some rules all people must obey for safety in our world today? What safety rules do you have in your family? Why are these rules important?

Witness WORDS

Noah

obedience

covenant

rainbow

Try this!

Make a rain gauge! Wash an empty jar, such as a jam or pickle jar. Use a permanent fine-tipped marker and a ruler to label the outside of the jar with incremental marks. Find an open location outside where you can leave the jar undisturbed. Keep a tally of the rainfall for each week or month. Record the information on a calendar.

SHOW

SHOW SERVICE

Has there been a weather-related natural disaster in the world lately? If so, use a map to show your child where the location is in reference to where you live. Find out how your family can offer help to the people who are living in that area. Consider collecting money, clothing, or blankets to send to them. Include the people in your family prayers.

Family Prayer

God, we thank you for giving us each other, and for giving us a beautiful world in which to live. Help us learn how to care for the world and for each other, and to always remember you keep your promises to us. **Amen**

Taking Care of God's Earth

An important word for Christians is stewardship. *Stewardship* is the way we manage our lives, our time, and everything God has given to us.

Are you a good steward?

How do you care for your body?

____

How do you care for the things you own?

____

List ways that you care for the earth:

I care for the earth…

at home:

____

at school:

____

in my community:

____

Crack the Code!

Decode this Bible verse by numbering the letters of the alphabet 1-26 (A = 1). Then write your favorite Bible verse or another special message in code and see if a friend can crack it!

7·15·4 • 19·1·23 • 5·22·5·18·25·20·8·9·14·7 • 20·8·1·20 • 8·5 • 8·1·4

13·1·4·5, • 1·14·4 • 9·14·4·5·5·4, • 9·20 • 23·1·19 • 22·5·18·25 • 7·15·15·4.

Genesis 1:31

Witness at Home!

Use these activities to nurture and celebrate faith at home.

KNOW

KNOW THE STORY

Ask your child to tell you the story of God's creation of the world. What did God say when each portion of creation was complete? (*It is good.*) Talk with your child about your favorite creature in God's world. What is his or her favorite creature? Why?

GROW

GROW IN FAITH

God's orderly work can be comforting as we read and reread the creation story. Whenever we spend time in nature, we can delight in the variety of God's handiwork. We can also take comfort in knowing that after all of the work of creation, God rested. It is important for our own faith growth that we honor God's plan and include a day of rest in our weekly lives.

Witness WORDS

creation

thanksgiving

stewardship

Try this!

Make a terrarium! Begin with a clean, wide-mouthed jar. Spread a thin layer of gravel or pebbles on the bottom. Add a layer of potting soil. Carefully position small plants in the soil. Add rocks or bark for interest. Mist the plants with water, or add water droplets. Cover with a lid or plastic wrap secured with a rubber band. Condensation will keep this mini-world moist. Periodically remove the lid for soil to dry, then water again.

SHOW

SHOW SERVICE

Talk with your child about the word *stewardship.* What does it mean to be a good steward? How can we be good stewards of all that God gives us? God gives us many gifts, including the gift of our body. How can you and your family take better care of this gift from God?

Family Prayer

Thank you, God, for this beautiful world that you created! We love to spend time outside, especially when we *(add a favorite family activity here)*. Help us remember to always care for the things you give us, especially our bodies!
Amen

